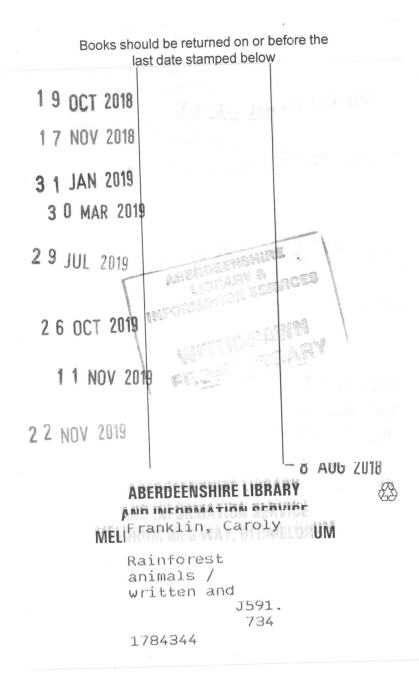

# World of Wonder
# RAINFOREST
# ANIMALS

The **golden potto** lives
in African rainforests.
At night it feeds on
insects by picking them
off twigs and leaves, or by
catching them as they fly past.

# SALARIYA

Published in Great Britain in 2007
by Book House, an imprint of
**The Salariya Book Company Ltd**
25 Marlborough Place,
Brighton BN1 1UB

*Author and artist:* Carolyn Franklin is
a graduate of Brighton College of Art,
England, specialising in design and
illustration. She has worked in animation
and advertising, and has written and
illustrated many natural-history books
for children.

*Editor:* Stephen Haynes

HB ISBN: 978-1-905638-26-0
PB ISBN: 978-1-905638-27-7

A CIP catalogue record for this book is
available from the British Library.

Printed and bound in China.
Printed on paper from
sustainable sources.

Visit our website at **www.book-house.co.uk**
for **free** electronic versions of:
**You Wouldn't Want to be an Egyptian Mummy!**
**You Wouldn't Want to be a Roman Gladiator!**
**Avoid Joining Shackleton's Polar Expedition!**
**Avoid Sailing on a 19th-Century Whaling Ship!**

# World of Wonder
# Rainforest Animals

Written and illustrated by
Carolyn Franklin

Squirrel monkey

# Contents

Green tree frog

# What is a rainforest?

A rainforest is a forest of trees which grow very close together, in a part of the world where it is warm and there is a lot of rain. Many amazing plants and animals live in the rainforests.

A rainforest can be divided into four layers: the **forest floor**, the **understorey**, the **canopy** and the **emergent layer**. Different plants grow on each layer, and these plants support many different animals.

Emergent layer

Canopy

Understorey

Forest floor

Cardinal
tetra

Swordtail

Silver
dollar

Electric eel

# Do fish live in rainforests?

Yes: over 1,500 different types of fish live in the River Amazon, which flows through the South American rainforests. There are tiny, brightly coloured fish called **tetra**, huge **stingrays** and giant **catfish**.

Neon
tetra

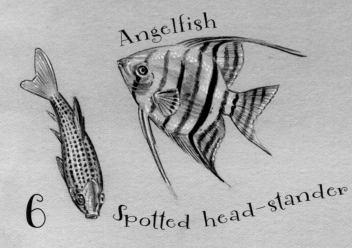

Angelfish

Spotted head-stander

The largest hunter in the River Amazon is the **black caiman**, a kind of alligator. It will grab, then drown and finally swallow its prey whole.

# Scary fish!

**Red piranha** hunt in large groups,
feeding mainly on other fish. However,
if a big land animal becomes stuck in the
water, a shoal of piranha will attack it,
eating everything but its bones.

Red-tailed catfish

Red piranha

Stingray

Chocolate cichlid

Mata-mata turtle

Hoatzin

## Smelly birds

Hoatzin are birds that live in thick forest near rivers and lakes. They only eat leaves, and this bulky diet not only makes it difficult for them to fly, but also makes them smell!

# Can a tapir snorkel?

A **tapir** has a snout rather like an elephant's trunk, which it uses for reaching and pulling plants into its mouth. When frightened, it can hide under the water and use its snout like a snorkel.

Alligator

Tapir

Paca

Anaconda

9

The **goliath bird-eating spider** really does eat small birds! It will also feed on frogs, large insects, lizards and even small mammals.

# How big is the largest spider?

The dark forest floor, covered in dead and dying leaves, is home to all sorts of **ants**, **termites**, **millipedes, beetles**, **worms** and **spiders**. The largest spider in the world is the goliath bird-eating spider – it can be as big as a dinner plate!

10

# Millipede

## True or False?
Leafcutter ants use the pieces of leaf that they cut to make tents.

Answers on page 31

## How many legs?
Most millipedes have between 80 and 400 legs. As they get older they may grow more legs.

Leafcutter ants

# Why are the tree roots so big?

The layer of soil in a rainforest is thin, so tree roots cannot grow deep down into the ground. Instead, the trees have big **buttress roots** that grow out from the side of their trunk and help hold the enormous trees in place.

## True or False?
Rainforests contain more than half of the world's huge number of plant and animal species.

Answers on page 31

Hummingbird

Postman butterfly

Tamandua

Hummingbird

Armadillo

Vine

Creeper

## Creepers!

Long, thin **creepers**, **vines** and **lianas** grow up towards the sunlit canopy, using the large trees for support.

Liana

Buttress roots

Coati

13

*Three-toed sloth*

## Do sloths go green?

The three-toed sloth uses its strong claws to cling upside down in the branches of the canopy. Tiny plants, too small to see, grow in the sloth's damp fur, making it look slightly green.

# Keel-billed toucan

Answers on page 31

## True or False?

A tree porcupine has a special tail which it waves in the air to keep itself cool. **?**

## Sounds like a frog!

A keel-billed toucan makes a sound just like a frog. Toucans eat mainly fruit, but they also eat lizards, snakes and even the eggs of smaller birds.

## Tree porcupine

15

# Do snakes eat birds?

**A**n **emerald tree boa** is a large, green snake. Boas don't have teeth for chewing, so they swallow birds and other prey whole!

Jaguar

## One bite!

A jaguar has very strong jaws and kills its prey with one bite. It will climb up into a tree, then pounce on its prey from a hiding place amongst the branches. Jaguars have powerful muscles, and long claws on their front paws.

Emerald tree boa

Blue tanager

# Can frogs live in trees?

Yes! High up in the branches of rainforest trees live tiny **poison-arrow frogs**.

## Bromeliad

Special plants called **bromeliads** growing in the canopy hold pools of rainwater in their leaves. Poison-arrow frogs carry their tadpoles to the pools to feed.

Dragonfly

Clearwing moth

The rainforest canopy towers as high as 45 metres above the ground. Where the leaves are less thick, the bright sunshine helps plants like ferns and mosses to grow on the tree branches.

Fern

Moss

Poison-arrow frog

Tadpoles

# How big is a monkey family?

Large groups of up to 300 **squirrel monkeys** may live together. The group will spread through the different levels of the forest to search for food.

True or False?
A harpy eagle eats monkeys, but prefers to catch sloths.

Answers on page 31

squirrel monkey

Macaw

Harpy eagle

## Which monkeys have red faces?

The **red uakari** is a monkey with a bright red face and head. These shy animals live in the forest canopy, eating seeds and nuts with their strong jaws.

Red uakari

21

Woolly monkey

# What lives in the tallest trees?

The tallest trees, called **emergents**, grow high above the thick, dark canopy. At over 60 metres tall, they are home to many types of birds, bats and monkeys.

Vultures have good senses of smell and sight, and can spot prey in the forest far below. Vultures prefer to eat animals that are already dead or even rotting!

King vultures

True or False?
20% of the world's bird species live in the trees of the Amazonian rainforest.

?

?

?

Answers on page 31

Vine snake

Hummingbird

Fragrant orchid

Bat

Instead of growing colourful leaves or petals, some plants produce strong smells. At night their scent attracts **fruit bats** and insects such as night-flying moths.

# Do animals hunt at night?

Yes! Many animals, such as the **owl monkey**, certain bats, sloths and insects, sleep during the day. Then at dusk they wake up and go in search of food. The owl monkey has enormous eyes which help it see in the dark.

Hawk moth

Owl monkey

Red-eyed
tree frog

25

# Do people live in rainforests?

Yes: for thousands of years people have lived in rainforests. The **Yanomami Indians** still live in parts of the South American rainforest. They use spears, longbows and poison-tipped arrows to catch fish, monkeys and wild pigs. They also grow plantains, which are similar to bananas.

The Yanomami live in hundreds of small villages dotted around the Amazon rainforest. Their homes are large, palm-covered huts which they share with other families. The forest provides them with all they need to live.

Quetzal

Orange-winged Amazon Parrot

True or False?
The Yanomami people put poison made from berries on the tips of their arrows.

?          ?

Answers on page 31

27

# Will there always be rainforests?

Each year huge areas of rainforest are destroyed. Areas are cleared of trees so that crops can be grown, or roads and cities can be built. Trees are cut down because wood is needed, or because there is a useful mineral under the ground.

Red-eyed tree frog

Many types of frog live in the rainforests today. But if we continue to destroy the forests these frogs and many other incredible animals will also die.

Answers on page 31

## True or False?

Rainforests can stop parts of the world flooding.

**?**

Rainforests are very important. Many of their plants can be used as medicines. Without rainforests, the world's weather would change.

# Useful words

**Amazon** A huge river in South America. It is not the longest river in the world, but it is the one with the most water.

**Bromeliads** A family of plants which includes the pineapple.

**Buttress roots** Roots that grow out sideways from the trunk of a tree to help support it in thin soil.

**Canopy** The second-highest part of the forest, where the branches of all but the very tallest trees are.

**Emergent** A very tall tree which grows above the forest canopy.

**Forest floor** The lowest level of the rainforest, where many insects and other creatures live amongst the decaying leaves.

Fer-de-lance

**Prey** Animals that are killed and eaten by other animals.

**Species** The name that scientists use to refer to an individual type of plant or animal.

**Tadpole** A baby frog.

**Understorey** The second-lowest level of the forest, formed by small trees and shrubs.

The fer-de-lance is the most dangerous snake found in the South American rainforest.

A chameleon
from Africa
shoots out
a long
tongue to
trap its prey.

# Answers

**Page 11  FALSE!** The leafcutter ants chew off pieces of leaf, which they carry to their underground nests. There they build 'compost heaps' on which fungus grows. Finally they feed this to their young.

**Page 12  TRUE!** Rainforests cover only a very tiny part (6% or less) of the Earth's surface, yet more than half of the world's different types of plants and animals can be found in these incredible forests.

**Page 15  FALSE!** The tree porcupine uses its special tail when climbing trees. If attacked, the porcupine may bite back, or sit down and shake its sharp quills at its enemy. Or it might stamp its feet and then roll up into a ball for protection.

**Page 20  TRUE!** Harpy eagles fly over the canopy snatching monkeys, lizards and sloths from the treetops.

**Page 23  TRUE!** As many as 20% (one in five) of the world's bird species live in the tall rainforest trees that surround the River Amazon.

**Page 27  FALSE!** They use the deadly skin of poison-arrow frogs. Forest people put the poison on their arrow tips when they go hunting.

**Page 29  TRUE!** Plants store carbon dioxide gas, which makes the earth and the air around it hotter. Without this, the earth would get warmer and the ice at the North and South Poles would melt. Low-lying land would then flood.

# Index (Illustrations are shown in **bold type**.)